WORLD ALMANAC®
LIBRARY OF THE STATES

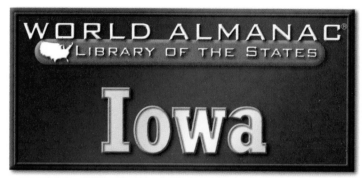

Iowa

THE HAWKEYE STATE

by Michael E. Martin

Curriculum Consultant: Jean Craven,
Director of Instructional Support,
Albuquerque, NM, Public Schools

WORLD ALMANAC® LIBRARY

Please visit our web site at: **www.worldalmanaclibrary.com**
For a free color catalog describing World Almanac® Library's
list of high-quality books and multimedia programs, call
1-800-848-2928 (USA) or 1-800-387-3178 (Canada).
World Almanac® Library's fax: (414) 332-3567.

Library of Congress Cataloging-in-Publication Data

Martin, Michael A.
    Iowa, the Hawkeye State / by Michael A. Martin.
      p. cm. — (World Almanac Library of the states)
    Includes bibliographical references and index.
    Summary: Presents the history, geography, people, politics
and government, economy, social life and customs, state events
and attractions, and notable people of Iowa.
    ISBN 0-8368-5133-1 (lib. bdg.)
    ISBN 0-8368-5303-2 (softcover)
    1. Iowa—Juvenile literature. [1. Iowa.] I. Title. II. Series.
F621.3.M36   2002
977.7—dc21   2002066389

This edition first published in 2002 by
World Almanac® Library
330 West Olive Street, Suite 100
Milwaukee, WI 53212 USA

This edition © 2002 by World Almanac® Library.

Design and Editorial: Bill SMITH STUDIO Inc.
Editor: Kristen Behrens
Assistant Editor: Megan Elias
Art Director: Olga Lamm
Photo Research: Sean Livingstone
World Almanac® Library Project Editor: Patricia Lantier
World Almanac® Library Editors: Monica Rausch, Catherine Gardner, Mary Dykstra
World Almanac® Library Production: Scott M. Krall, Tammy Gruenewald,
  Katherine A. Goedheer

Photo credits: pp. 4–5: © PhotoDisc; p. 6: (top, bottom) © PhotoDisc, (center) © Corel; p. 7: (top)
Courtesy of Iowa State University, (bottom) Dover; p. 9: Courtesy of the Library of Congress;
p. 10: © ArtToday; p. 11: Dover; p. 12: Courtesy of Iowa Tourism Office; p. 13: Courtesy of Library
of Congress; p. 14: © Francis Miller/TimePix; p. 15: Courtesy of the Iowa Tourism Office; p. 17:
© ArtToday; p. 18: © PhotoDisc; p. 19: Courtesy of the Iowa Tourism Office; p. 20: (left, right):
Courtesy of the Iowa Tourism Office, (center) © Corel; p. 21: (left, center): © PAINET INC., (right)
© PhotoDisc; p. 23: Courtesy of the Iowa Tourism Office; pp. 26–27: © PhotoDisc; p. 29: Courtesy
of the Iowa Tourism Office; p. 31: Courtesy of the Library of Congress; p. 32: © Charles
Peterson/TimePix; p. 33: Courtesy of the Iowa Tourism Office; p. 34: © PAINET INC.; p. 35:
© Brent Smith/Reuters/TimePix; pp. 36–37: Courtesy of the Iowa Tourism Office; pp. 38–39:
Dover; p. 40: © PhotoDisc; p. 41: © Dean Loomis/TimePix; pp. 42–43: Courtesy of the Library of
Congress; p. 44: Courtesy of the Iowa Tourism Office; p. 45: © PhotoDisc.

Printed in the United States of America

1 2 3 4 5 6 7 8 9 06 05 04 03 02

Iowa

Crossroads of Plenty

From its westward-rolling prairie lands to the hardwood forests of its eastern highlands, Iowa is a crossroads in many ways. Nestled in the heart of the Midwest, Iowa stands astride two different, yet complementary, worlds. Western Iowa is a realm of cornstalks — the pastoral farmland that Iowa's own Grant Wood captured in his classic paintings. The eastern part of the state is the urban domain of modern industry.

Ages ago, glaciers moving down from the frozen north deposited a deep, rich layer of topsoil across Iowa. The result was perfect farmland that has made the Hawkeye State famous for its agriculture. Iowa leads the nation in the production of corn and pork, and about 7 percent of the nation's food supply originates on Iowa's farms.

In Iowa, farming and manufacturing work hand in hand, as factories work to process Iowa's produce. Breakfast cereals, popcorn, corn oil, and cornstarch are just a few of the state's many products, while pork-processing and farm machinery manufacturing play strong roles in Iowa's economy.

Iowa also has a tradition of nurturing its residents both culturally and educationally. From its early days, the state has contributed scientists, political leaders, entrepreneurs, artists, writers, and entertainers to the national and international scenes. The roster of famous Iowans includes the nation's thirty-first president, Herbert Hoover; *The Music Man* composer Meredith Willson; and talk-show legend Johnny Carson. It is no surprise that Iowa also exerts a potent influence over the nation's political leadership. Every four years, the Hawkeye State hosts the unique Iowa Caucuses. These small political meetings help determine early on which candidates make it onto the ballot in the presidential race.

As Iowans look to the future, the crossroads state continues to foster both new and traditional ways of living, placing its small-town culture in harmony with high-tech development.

▶ Map of Iowa showing the interstate highway system, as well as major cities and waterways.

▼ Iowa is the top producer of corn in the United States.

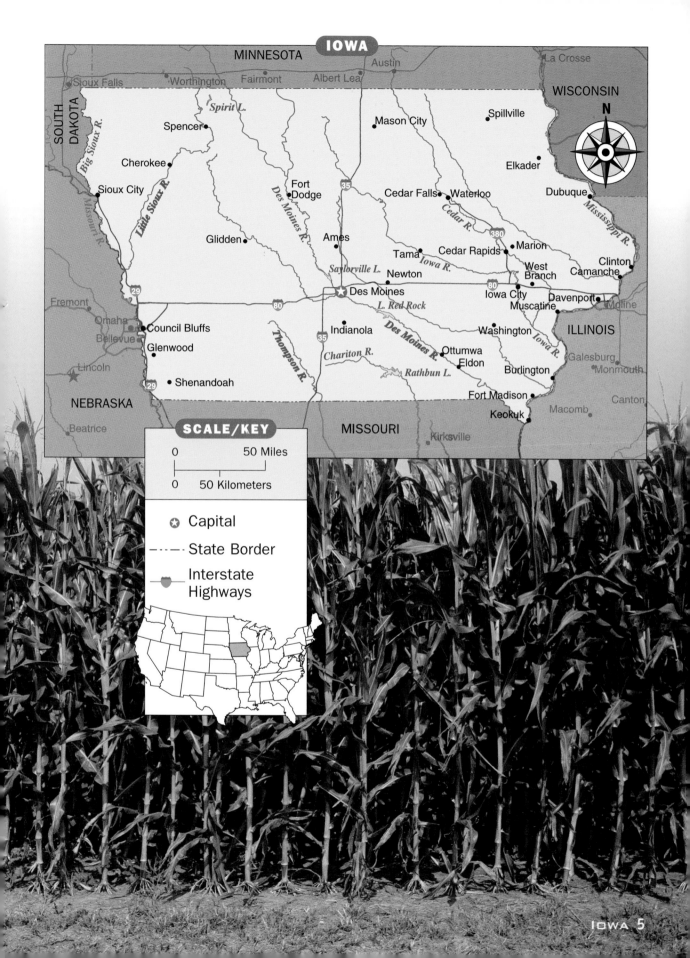

IOWA

MINNESOTA

WISCONSIN

SOUTH DAKOTA

Sioux Falls   *Worthington*   *Fairmont*   *Albert Lea*   *Austin*   *La Crosse*

Spirit L.

Spencer

Mason City   Spillville

Cherokee   Elkader

Big Sioux R.   Sioux City   Fort Dodge   Cedar Falls Waterloo   Dubuque

Little Sioux R.   *Des Moines R.*   35   *Mississippi R.*

Glidden   Ames   *Cedar R.*   380   Cedar Rapids Marion   Clinton

Missouri R.   Tama   *Iowa R.*   West Branch   Camanche

Saylorville L.   Newton   80

★ Des Moines   Iowa City   Davenport   Moline

Fremont   *L. Red Rock*   Muscatine

Omaha   29   Council Bluffs   Indianola   35   *Des Moines R.*   Washington   *Iowa R.*   ILLINOIS

Bellevue   Glenwood   *Thompson R.*   Ottumwa Eldon   *Galesburg*

Lincoln   *Chariton R.*   Burlington   *Monmouth*

• Shenandoah   *Rathbun L.*

29   Fort Madison   *Canton*

NEBRASKA   Keokuk   *Macomb*

Beatrice   MISSOURI   *Kirksville*

N

Fast Facts

IOWA

Iowa (IA), The Hawkeye State

Entered Union

December 28, 1846 (29th state)

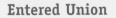

Capital	Population
Des Moines	198,682

Total Population (2000)

2,926,324 (30th most populous state) — *Between 1990 and 2000, the population of Iowa increased 5.4 percent.*

Largest Cities	Population
Des Moines	198,682
Cedar Rapids	120,758
Davenport	98,359
Sioux City	85,013
Waterloo	68,747
Iowa City	62,220
Council Bluffs	58,268
Dubuque	57,686

Land Area

55,869 square miles (144,701 square kilometers) (23rd largest state)

State Motto

"Our Liberties We Prize, and Our Rights We Will Maintain."

State Song

"The Song of Iowa," *sung to the melody of "Der Tannenbaum," with words by S. H. M. Byers, adopted in 1911.*

State Bird

Eastern goldfinch — *Also known as the wild canary or the American goldfinch, the eastern goldfinch is often seen in Iowa and frequently remains in the state even during the harsh winters.*

State Tree

Oak — *Iowa's abundant oak trees provide habitat for many species of animals and birds. The oak provides timber as well as sustenance, in the form of acorns, for blue jays, chipmunks, deer, grackles, nuthatches, pheasants, raccoons, quail, squirrels, wild turkeys, wood ducks, woodpeckers, and other wild creatures. The oak became Iowa's official state tree in 1961.*

State Flower

Wild rose — *The wild prairie rose displays its pink blooms from June until late in the summer. In 1897, this flower was chosen to decorate the silver service the Hawkeye State presented to its namesake battleship, the USS Iowa.*

State Rock

Geode — *This spherical, usually hollow rock is lined with crystals. Iowa has long been known as possessing a relative abundance of these rare and beautiful rocks.*

PLACES TO VISIT

Devonian Fossil Gorge, *Coralville Lake*
The torrential floods of 1993 ripped a 15-foot (4.6-meter) gorge into the earth near Coralville Lake, exposing an ancient fossil seabed dating to the Devonian period. Visitors can gaze back to when fish were the most advanced life-forms on Earth.

Herbert Hoover's birthplace, *West Branch*
Surrounded by a park, this historic site honors the thirty-first U.S. president. Visitors can see the two-room Quaker cottage where Hoover was born.

Ledges State Park, *near Ames*
With its abundance of woodlands and prairies, Ledges State Park is a favorite of nature lovers. The park also preserves artifacts made during the region's four thousand years of human habitation.

For other places and events, see p. 44.

BIGGEST, BEST, AND MOST

- Iowa is home to the nation's shortest and steepest scenic railway. Located in Dubuque, the track is known as the Fenelon Place Elevator.

- The Hawkeye State ranks first nationally in the production of corn and pork and is also a leading producer of beef, soybeans, and grain.

- A farm near East Peru was the birthplace of the country's best-selling variety of apple: the Red Delicious. During the 1880s, Iowan Jesse Hiatt discovered shoots growing from the stump of a wild apple tree on his land.

STATE FIRSTS

- **1854** Grinnell College grants first bachelor of arts degrees west of the Mississippi.
- **1869** Iowa native Arabella Babb Mansfield becomes the first U.S. woman to be permitted to practice law.
- **1917** Merle Hay of Glidden becomes one of the first three Americans to die in World War I.

Iowa Ingenuity

In 1939, Iowa State University professor John V. Atanasoff and graduate student Clifford Berry built the world's first electronic digital computer. Atanasoff left the university and went to work for the U.S. government after the outbreak of World War II, and other scientists and engineers developed the Atanasoff-Berry designs into the first generation of computers. Atanasoff and Berry were finally given credit for their world-changing invention in 1973.

Iowa's Nicknames

Iowa's most often-used nickname is the Hawkeye State, a term that is probably derived from the name of Black Hawk, a Native American chief. In 1832, Black Hawk led the Sauk and Fox Indians in war to reclaim land they had held. The U.S. Army defeated Black Hawk's forces and pushed them off a large tract of land running alongside the Mississippi River, a region that later became known as the Black Hawk Purchase. The Black Hawk Purchase became the site of some of Iowa's earliest large-scale permanent settlements in 1833. After Iowa became known for its prodigious corn production during the 1850s, the state was also sometimes referred to as the Corn State.

Splendor in the Grasslands

Taking this Territory, all in all, for convenience and navigation, water, fuel, and timber; for richness of soil; for beauty of appearance, and for pleasantness of climate, it surpasses any portion of the United States with which I am acquainted.

— *Lieutenant Albert M. Lea, U.S. Army, 1835*

People first entered the land now known as Iowa as far back as 11,000 B.C., after the glaciers of the last ice age melted. These early inhabitants hunted animals for food. Over the millennia, these ancient Iowans were eventually joined by others, and they began to build villages. By about 500 B.C., a group known collectively as the Woodland peoples began to emerge. The Woodland period lasted until about A.D. 1000. Over the centuries, the Woodland peoples developed and used technologies that enabled them to grow crops more efficiently and to produce more sophisticated types of pottery. They also constructed large mounds that were used for burial. More than one thousand of these mounds can still be seen in present-day Iowa. Northeastern Iowa was home to a native population known as the Effigy Mound culture from about A.D. 650 to 1000. This culture was unusual in that it built mounds in animal shapes. Examples of these mounds, along with mounds built by other peoples, can be seen at Effigy Mounds National Monument in Harper's Ferry. The Effigy Mound and Woodland cultures gradually gave way to the Plains Village, Mill Creek, Central Plains, and Oneota cultures. Each developed distinctive building styles as well as food cultivation and storage systems. The Oneota are probably the ancestors of the Ioway, Oto, Missouri, and Winnebago tribes.

By the time Europeans began exploring Iowa in the 1670s, the region's southeastern area was home to the Illinois people, while the rest of the territory was controlled by peoples of the Great Plains. These included the Ioway, Omaha, Oto, Missouri, and Ottawa. They hunted the area's vast herds of buffalo for food, clothing, and shelter. Dakota

Native Americans of Iowa
Dakota (Sioux)
Illinois
Ioway
Mesquakie (Fox)
Miami
Missouri
Omaha
Oto
Ottawa
Sauk
Winnebago

(Sioux) hunting parties from as far west as what are now the Dakotas made occasional forays into Iowa as well. From around 1750 until the early nineteenth century, European settlement in the more eastern regions of North America displaced many Native peoples. Settlers pushed the Sauk and Mesquakie (Fox) peoples of Wisconsin into Iowa. The Sauk and Mesquakie settled in the eastern and southern portions of Iowa, on land they seized from the Ioway people.

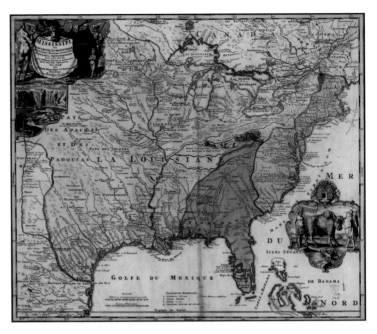

European Exploration and Settlement

In June 1673, the French explorer Louis Jolliet and missionary Jacques Marquette paddled their canoes down the Wisconsin River into the Mississippi River. Although they were the first Europeans to see Iowa, their visits were mainly intended to learn about the territory and had little immediate impact either on the land or the people who lived there. In 1680, French explorer René-Robert Cavelier, Sieur de La Salle, dispatched Michel Aco and missionary Louis Hennepin on a mission to explore the upper Mississippi River, where they passed Iowa's eastern shore. By 1682, Iowa was part of the sprawling French holdings known as the Louisiana Territory, a region claimed by La Salle for France's King Louis XIV.

Around 1690, Nicholas Perrot taught the Miami how to mine lead near the site of the present-day city of Dubuque. For the next five decades, however, the French did very little with Iowa, which was visited only by a few fur traders, trappers, and soldiers. France established no permanent Iowa settlements and, by 1762, had handed their North American lands west of the Mississippi River over to Spain. French-Canadian Julien Dubuque received permission from the Mesquakie to mine lead and became Iowa's first European settler in 1788. In 1796, he was awarded a Spanish land grant. Some trappers and hunters soon took up residence there. In 1800, Spain gave the Louisiana Territory back to France.

DID YOU KNOW?

The name *Iowa* has several different possible meanings. By some accounts, it is named for the Iowa River region, which in turn was described by an Ioway word that means "beautiful land," "this is the place," or "here I rest." It is also possible that *Iowa* is actually a misspelling of the Indian word *ayuxwa*, which translates to "drowsy one" or "one who puts to sleep."

With the Louisiana Purchase of 1803, Napoleon Bonaparte sold the Louisiana Territory to the United States to raise money for France's war in Europe. The next year, on the order of President Thomas Jefferson, Meriwether Lewis and William Clark navigated the Missouri River as the first leg of an epic two-year exploration of these newly acquired lands. Charles Floyd, a member of the Lewis and Clark expedition, died during the journey near present-day Sioux City. The only man to lose his life on this bold mission to cross the continent, Floyd was buried in Iowa. The intrepid Zebulon M. Pike explored the region further in 1805 and 1806, scouting the upper Mississippi in preparation for the establishment of military outposts, such as Fort Madison, which was founded in 1808. Still more explorers soon followed to fill in the blanks left by Lewis and Clark and Zebulon Pike. Albert M. Lea, Stephen H. Long, Henry R. Schoolcraft, and Stephen W. Kearny mapped Iowa for a fresh wave of soldiers and settlers.

▲ A contemporary drawing depicting soldiers engaged in battle during the Black Hawk War.

The U.S. Territorial Period

During its earliest years as a U.S. territory, control of the region that is now Iowa changed hands several times. The region was first governed by the Territory of Indiana. This ended in 1805, when the area was officially made part of the Territory of Louisiana. In 1812, present-day Iowa was attached to the Territory of Missouri, but when Missouri entered the Union in 1821, the area was briefly left "unorganized," with no formal territorial government.

Although a few military and fur-trading outposts had been established, the government declared the region officially off-limits to permanent settlement and reserved its lands for those Native Americans who had been pushed out of Illinois. This situation changed after 1832, when Sauk chief Black Hawk led the Sauk and Mesquakie in an attempt to regain their land in Illinois. The U.S. Army eventually defeated Black Hawk. The Black Hawk War, as it was called, effectively

Winter of Discontent at Spirit Lake

Relations between Iowa's settlers and its Native peoples were generally good, but there were exceptions. During the winter of 1857, Dakota (Sioux) leader Inkpaduta learned that European settlers had built houses along the shores of Spirit Lake, a place Native peoples saw as sacred. Inkpaduta and his warriors raided the area, killing more than thirty and kidnapping four women. Abbie Gardner, whose family died in the raid, was one of the captives. Eventually set free, she wrote an account of her time among the Native Americans.

ended organized resistance to non-Native settlement in Iowa. The U.S. government then made a 50-mile (80-km) strip of Mississippi River land available to pioneers. This region, known as the Black Hawk Purchase, sprouted its first official U.S. settlement in 1833. After brief periods of the region being part of the Michigan and then the Wisconsin territories, Congress made Iowa into its own territory on July 4, 1838. The Iowa Territory included all of the modern state as well as most of the Dakotas and Minnesota. Democrat and former Ohio governor Robert Lucas became Iowa's first territorial governor, appointed by President Martin Van Buren. The first territorial capital was established in Burlington, then moved to Iowa City in 1841. As the government acquired more land from Native Americans throughout the 1830s and 1840s, new settlements sprang up across Iowa. The population rose steadily, and Iowa became the twenty-ninth state on December 28, 1846.

Population Grows

By 1851, all Native American-held Iowa land was under U.S. government control. Non-Native settlement drove the Mesquakie out of Iowa and into Kansas, but, in 1856, they returned to Iowa. They bought some 5 square miles (13 sq km) of land back from the state. This land, located near Tama along the Iowa River, is still under Mesquakie ownership today. Not all Native peoples took the Mesquakie approach, however. In 1857, a band of Sioux warriors massacred settlers at the western-Iowa settlement of Spirit Lake. This incident, however, did not slow down settlement; farmers and traders kept on streaming into Iowa from eastern states. By 1850, Iowa's population had reached about 192,000; a decade later, this figure had swelled to around 675,000.

Civil War

Most of Iowa's swiftly expanding population was solidly against slavery, the major issue leading up to the U.S. Civil War (1861–1865). Although no

Zebulon Pike: Bad Luck Adventurer

Only the hardiest explorers and adventurers braved the United States's inland wilderness. One of these was Zebulon Montgomery Pike (1779-1813), an army officer. Pike's earliest mission of discovery, in 1805, took him to the upper Mississippi River, following present-day Iowa's eastern border. Pike investigated the Mississippi's source and purchased land for military outposts from the local Native peoples.

In 1806, Pike explored the Arkansas and Red Rivers in what is now Oklahoma. In southeastern Colorado, Pike and his freezing, starving party tried and failed to climb a snow-covered mountain that is now known as Pikes Peak. Pike's wanderings eventually led him to the Rio Grande — and to capture by Spanish troops.

Civil War battles were actually fought within Iowa's borders, the Hawkeye State sent nearly 80,000 of its sons to fight for the Union cause, a larger percentage of its people than any other Union state. The bitter conflict transformed politics in Iowa, a long-time Democratic party stronghold. Distressed by the Democrats' failure to condemn slavery, a majority of Iowans voted Republican in the 1856 election. In 1860 and 1864, Iowa voters favored the Republican candidate, Abraham Lincoln. Many people who opposed slavery, called abolitionists, also actively participated in the Underground Railroad, which secretly helped fleeing slaves reach freedom in northern states and Canada. After the war's end, Iowa allowed African-American children to attend its public schools and gave African-American men the right to vote.

Getting from Here to There

During the post-Civil War years, the growth of Iowa's transportation network kept pace with its exploding population, resulting in an even distribution of people across the mostly rural state. Shipping goods by steamboat became a huge industry along the Mississippi River between 1850 and 1870. By the time the first trans-Iowa railroad appeared in 1867, many of Iowa's small towns had grown rich. By 1870, four different railroads crossed the state. Those towns able to ship their products both by rail and by river fared doubly well during these economic boom times.

Underground Railroad

Many Iowa abolitionists, or opponents of slavery, operated "stations" on the Underground Railroad. These stations were houses or other places where slaves escaping north to freedom (usually to Canada) could stop and rest, safe from anyone who might turn them over to the authorities. They hid in basements, closets, and even crawl spaces as they made their slow, treacherous journey, communicating in code by using songs, quilt patterns, and even dance steps.

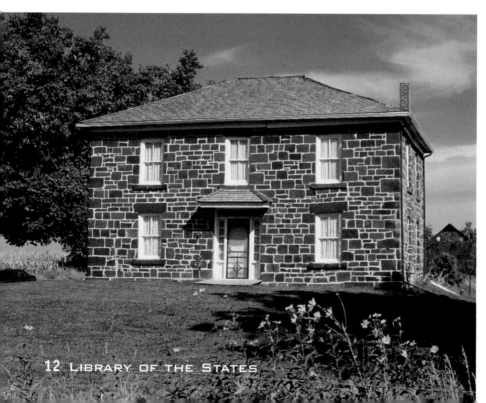

◀ The George B. Hitchcock House in Lewis was one of many Iowa houses that were stops on the Underground Railroad.

Farmers Unite!

Not everyone shared in the economic bonanza, however. The vast majority of Iowan families were land-owning commercial farmers who had to contend with depressed markets for their crops as well as pests, frequent droughts, and floods. Railroad companies made matters worse by charging excessive freight fees for Iowa's agricultural goods. Iowa's growers responded by banding together to form a state Grange organization to address these concerns. The Iowa Grange supported a group known as the Anti-Monopoly party, which gained control of the Iowa legislature in 1873. The following year, the legislature passed the Granger Laws, which regulated railroad shipping rates. The railroad industry managed to get these laws repealed in 1878. A state commission later negotiated shipping rates that both the railroads and the farmers could accept. As the nineteenth century drew to a close, Iowa's farmers further improved their fortunes by diversifying from wheat cultivation into feed corn, with which they fattened their hogs for the urban livestock markets.

▲ Advertisements such as this 1872 flier lured settlers to Iowa in the late 1800s, promising them cheap land and easy credit.

Transformation in the Twentieth Century

The Eighteenth Amendment to the U.S. Constitution, which made the manufacture, sale, and transportation of alcoholic beverages illegal, was ratified in 1919. The period during which this amendment was in force, from 1919 to 1933, was known as Prohibition. Decades earlier, in 1855, Iowa had enacted similar laws in response to the state's strong temperance, or anti-alcohol, sentiments. Territorial Governor Robert Lucas had supported the temperance movement as far back as the 1830s. In 1885, Iowa's legislature passed an even stricter ban on alcohol. This law was later softened, then removed from the books altogether in 1915, four years before national prohibition began. After Prohibition, the Iowa legislature began eliminating the state's restrictions on the sale of alcoholic beverages.

As the twentieth century began, the nation as a whole began to move from an agriculture-based economy toward one based on manufacturing. Farming continued to be important in Iowa, however. Between 1870 and 1920, Iowa's farms fed much of the growing country. The productivity of Iowa's farms increased exponentially due to such innovations as the internal combustion engine and, in the 1920s, high-yield, hybrid strains of corn. Automobiles and trucks made it easier for farmers to bring their products to market in the larger towns. Meanwhile, the eastern, industrial part of the state enjoyed a manufacturing boom, becoming a prime source of tractors and other farm machinery.

World War I — and the Aftermath

In 1917, when the United States entered World War I, some 113,000 Iowans left the towns and cornfields to join the fight in Europe. One of the first three American soldiers killed in that conflict was Private Merle Hay of Glidden, whose memorial stands today in France, where he fell in battle. During the war, rising prices for Iowa farmland forced many farmers to borrow heavily to acquire new land. When the Great Depression began in 1929, many of these farmers were strangled by debt. They were not able to keep up their loan payments, and their land was taken away by the lenders. Federal legislation championed by President Franklin D. Roosevelt in the mid-1930s helped bail out some of Iowa's hardest-hit farmers. The growers themselves also took steps to improve their situation. They began banding together into farm cooperatives to cut costs, increase their

▼ An Iowa farmer inspects his corn crop. Iowa's produce helped feed U.S. troops and citizens as well as the nation's European allies during World War II.

buying power, and gain leverage in the markets for their goods. Without the Roosevelt-era laws and the farm cooperatives, many more Iowans would have lost their land.

▲ A riverboat casino cruises on the Missouri River.

World War II and Beyond

During the United States's World War II years (1941–1945), Hawkeye State farmers prospered as a result of the huge demand the war created for corn and pork products. Thousands of Iowans marched off to war, and the USS *Iowa*, one of four "Iowa Class" battleships, saw service in the Pacific Ocean. Following the war and into the 1960s, manufacturing and food-processing industries flocked to Iowa. This industrial influx quickly moved Iowa away from its traditional farm-based economy and carried the state into the age of heavy industry. Farm consolidation and increased agricultural automation forced people to leave agricultural jobs and head to the cities to find industrial jobs. According to the 1960 U.S. Census, 53 percent of Iowans were living in towns and cities rather than on farms — a drastic shift in Iowa's way of life.

Recent Years

By the middle of the 1970s, manufacturing was generating more dollars than farming. During the early 1980s, farmers suffered from low crop prices, a global food surplus, and high interest rates. Many were forced out of business, and, as a result, many rural banks closed. This was also an era when the government was reducing price supports, which guarantee price levels for certain crops. All of these factors caused farmland to lose value. Farmers had to find other jobs to stay afloat. This agricultural slump also harmed suppliers of seed, fertilizer, and machinery. Many of Iowa's young people began leaving Iowa in search of brighter opportunities elsewhere. Fortunately for the rural Iowans who stayed behind, the farm slump leveled out toward the end of the 1980s. Today manufacturing, service industries, tourism, and riverboat gambling (legalized in 1989) have increased in importance. Farming, however, is still fundamental to Iowa's identity.

Five of Iowa's Bravest Sons

Many Iowans saw action in World War II, including five brothers from Waterloo. Eager to serve, the Sullivan brothers — Albert, Francis, George, Joseph, and Madison — joined the U.S. Navy. By 1942, all five were serving on the same warship, the USS *Juneau*. On November 13 of that year, the *Juneau* sank during fighting in the South Pacific, and the Sullivan brothers were killed. After this tragedy, the U.S. War Department prohibited members of the same family from serving together. To honor the brothers, the navy named two vessels for them, and the city of Waterloo christened its main convention site the Five Sullivan Brothers Convention Center.

From Rural to Urban

> I'm looking rather seedy now while holding down my claim,
> And my vittles are not always the best;
> And the mice play shyly 'round me as I nestle down to rest
> In my little old sod shanty on the plain.
>
> *— from the folk tune "Little Old Sod Shanty on the Plain,"*
> *circa 1862*

For all the stunning population growth of its early years, the Iowa of today is relatively sparsely populated. While it is an average state in terms of size (it places twenty-third among the states in land area), Iowa ranks thirtieth in number of people, with a population of 2,926,324, according to the 2000 U.S. Census. There are 52.4 people per square mile (20 people per sq km) in Iowa compared to the nationwide average of 79.6 (31 per sq km). One reason for the relatively small population is a modern trend toward migration out of the state. Iowa shows signs of recovering from the economic slump of the 1980s, which drove people from the state and led to a 5 percent decline in the number of Iowans. The population increased at a rate of 5.4 percent over the last decade, but this is less than half the national rate of increase.

Age Distribution in Iowa
(2000 Census)

0–4	188,413
5–19	639,570
20–24	203,663
25–44	808,259
45–64	650,206
65 & over	436,213

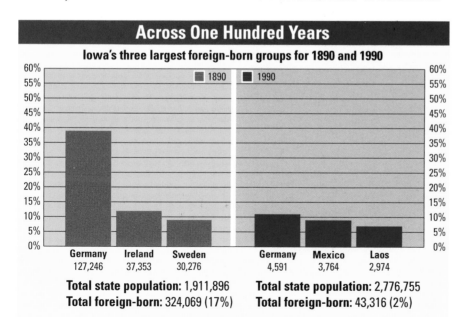

Across One Hundred Years
Iowa's three largest foreign-born groups for 1890 and 1990

■ 1890   ■ 1990

| Germany 127,246 | Ireland 37,353 | Sweden 30,276 | Germany 4,591 | Mexico 3,764 | Laos 2,974 |

Total state population: 1,911,896
Total foreign-born: 324,069 (17%)

Total state population: 2,776,755
Total foreign-born: 43,316 (2%)

Patterns of Immigration

The total number of people who immigrated to Iowa in 1998 was 1,655. Of that number, the largest immigrant groups were from Mexico (22.1%), Vietnam (13.2%), and India (7.8%).

An Immigrant Destination

In its early years, Iowa experienced a population boom. Immediately following the opening of the Black Hawk Purchase in 1833, settlers flocked to Iowa from the eastern states, mainly New York and Ohio. Immigrants arrived from such European countries as Bohemia (now part of the Czech Republic), Denmark, England, Ireland, the Netherlands, Germany, Norway, Sweden, and Switzerland. By 1870, almost 20 percent of Iowa's residents were foreign-born.

▲ Early immigrants to Iowa made their way across the state in covered wagons.

Ethnic Profile

Almost 93 percent of modern Iowa's population can be described as non-Hispanic Caucasians. Approximately 35 percent of Iowans are descended from Germans, the largest of Iowa's nineteenth-century immigrant groups. German-speaking communities exist today in what are known as the Amana Colonies and among the state's Amish villages in Washington and Johnson Counties. Some 98 percent of modern Iowans were born in the United States. Only 2.1 percent of Iowa's population is African American, which is far less than the national average of 12.3 percent. Regardless, African Americans form one of the state's largest minority groups.

DID YOU KNOW?

About 80 percent of Iowans were born within the Hawkeye State. Only around 2 percent were born in foreign countries.

Heritage and Background, Iowa — Year 2000

▶ Here's a look at the racial backgrounds of Iowans today. Iowa ranks forty-first among all U.S. states with regard to African Americans as a percentage of the population.

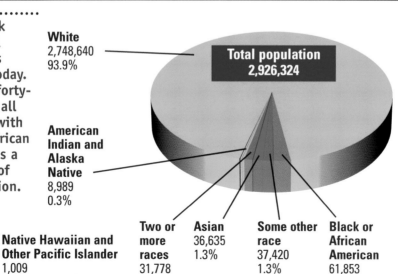

White
2,748,640
93.9%

**Total population
2,926,324**

American Indian and Alaska Native
8,989
0.3%

Native Hawaiian and Other Pacific Islander
1,009
Less than 0.1%

Two or more races
31,778
1.1%

Asian
36,635
1.3%

Some other race
37,420
1.3%

Black or African American
61,853
2.1%

Note: 2.8% (82,473) of the population identify themselves as **Hispanic** or **Latino,** a cultural designation that crosses racial lines. Hispanics and Latinos are counted in this category as well as the racial category of their choice.

Education: A Sterling Tradition

Iowa has a superb history in education. Iowans have earned more undergraduate degrees per 100,000 people than has any other state's population. The U.S. Department of Labor reports that Iowa has the highest literacy rate in the nation. Among adults over the age of twenty-five, 88.4 percent hold high school diplomas, and 22.2 percent have either a bachelor's or an advanced college degree. Iowa also has some of the nation's finest schools, and the state is particularly strong in the elementary and secondary arenas.

In 1830, a physician named Isaac Galland opened Iowa's first public school near Keokuk in southeastern Iowa. Nine years later, Iowa's territorial legislature created Iowa's free public school system, and the state's first public library opened in 1853. The early 1930s saw the opening of the David W. Smouse Opportunity School in Des Moines — one of the nation's first public schools for children with disabilities.

Educational Levels of Iowa Workers (age 25 and over)

Less than 9th grade	83,620
9th to 12th grade, no diploma	130,175
High school graduate, including equivalency	688,491
Some college, no degree or associate degree	531,463
Bachelor's degree	281,893
Graduate or professional degree	127,960

▼ Des Moines, Iowa's capital as well as its largest city, sits on the Des Moines River.

Iowa is home to three state universities: the University of Iowa, noted for its fine arts institution, established in Iowa City in 1847; Iowa State University of Science and Technology, an agricultural and sciences school founded at Ames in 1858; and the University of Northern Iowa, which opened at Cedar Falls in 1876. The University of Iowa is world famous for its Writers' Workshop. In 1965, Iowa's General Assembly authorized the establishment of community colleges and vocational schools. Among Iowa's well-respected private institutions are Grinnell College in Grinnell and Drake University in Des Moines.

▲ The University of Iowa in Iowa City is world-renowned for its Writers' Workshop. The university also educates 80 percent of Iowa's dentists, 60 percent of its pharmacists, and 50 percent of its physicians.

Where Do Iowans Live?

In 1960, the U.S. Census recorded a significant change in Iowa's population; urban Iowans outnumbered their rural counterparts for the first time in history, lured from declining farms to urban manufacturing and service jobs. Today, a little more than half of Iowa's population lives in urban areas, although between 1990 and 2000, the percentage of Iowans who live in rural areas increased slightly. Iowa has one of the nation's largest farm populations, some 294,000 people. Iowa's most populous cities include Des Moines, Cedar Rapids, Davenport, Sioux City, Waterloo, Iowa City, Council Bluffs, and Dubuque. All of these cities have populations in excess of 50,000 people. Iowa's greatest density of Native Americans can be found in Tama County's Mesquakie Settlement. Muscatine and Louisa Counties contain Iowa's largest concentration of Hispanics.

By 2000, about 7.7 percent of Iowans were age 75 years or older, one of the nation's highest proportions of elderly people. Iowa's current median age is 36.6, slightly older than the national average of 35.3.

Religion

Nearly 90 percent of Iowa's population identify with one of the Christian denominations. Some 6 percent of Iowans are Baptists, around 4 percent are Presbyterians, and Lutherans and Methodists each account for about 15 percent of the total population. Catholics represent about 18 percent of the state's population. Iowa's Jewish populations tend to be clustered in larger cities. A large Muslim community lives in Cedar Rapids.

Seas of Grass Between the Rivers

> Rock River was beautiful country. I loved my towns, my cornfields, and the home of my people. It is yours now. Keep it as we did.
>
> — *Chief Black Hawk in his last public appearance on July 4, 1837*

When the last ice age reached its peak about 18,000 years ago, glaciers covered much of Iowa's land. The sheer weight of these ice masses flattened the region's sedimentary bedrock into level plains. As the glaciers melted, they left vast amounts of nutrient-rich soil, which wind and flowing water spread across the land. The highest point in glacier-flattened Iowa is in the northwest and tops out at 1,670 feet (509 m). The state's lowest point is 480 feet (146 m) above sea level in the southeast, near the Mississippi River. Some portions of ancient Iowa escaped the crushing force of the glaciers. A striking region of rocky bluffs and cliffs in northeastern Iowa is famous among avid hikers, who call it "Little Switzerland."

The Land and Its Resources

The key to Iowa's tremendous success as a farming state can be found in its lucky combination of a moist climate, a long growing season, and the dark prairie topsoil brought by the glaciers. Iowa possesses more of this prime growing soil than any other state. It covers about 90 percent of the state's total land area. The soil was in a thick layer when

Highest Point
Hawkeye Point
1,670 feet (509 m)
above sea level

▼ *From left to right:* the Mississippi River, which forms Iowa's eastern border; a peregrine falcon, the target of conservation efforts; windblown hills of western Iowa; wild sunflowers on an Iowa prairie; an Iowa barn; aerial view of Iowa farmland.

the state's early settlers began farming. As Iowa's farmers exposed more and more topsoil, however, much of it was carried away by water and wind, and the thick layer wore down to a thin skin. Farmers began employing special agricultural techniques, such as contour plowing, to slow erosion. Partly as a result of these practices, it is still possible to farm in Iowa without irrigation.

Climate

The Hawkeye State's climate is one of extremes, making for very hot summers and freezing winters. The collision of warm air from the Gulf of Mexico with colder weather systems from the Arctic or the Pacific Ocean brings plenty of rain and snow to Iowa. Average summer high temperatures are 75° Fahrenheit (24° Celsius) but are known to exceed 100°F (38°C). Summers in Iowa are not just hot; they're muggy. Temperatures vary so wildly in Iowa that they can rise or fall by as much as 50°F (28°C) in a single day! Iowa's lowest recorded temperature, -47°F (-44°C), occurred on February 3, 1996, at Elkader. The record high, 118°F (48°C), was set on July 20, 1934, at Keokuk. Although it has extremes, the climate produces a long growing season — 150 days — and plenty of water for crops.

Water: A Land Bounded by Rivers

Iowa's borders are formed by the Mississippi River on the east and the Missouri River on the west, two of the nation's most vital waterways. The Big Sioux River forms the northern third of Iowa's western border. Several other rivers flow through the state's interior as well. They provide hydroelectric power and transportation to the main river arteries flanking the state. Located in central Iowa, the Des Moines River is one of the largest internal water transportation corridors and is responsible for almost

Average January temperature
Cedar Rapids: 18°F (-7.8°C)
Sioux City: 27.6°F (-2.4°C)

Average July temperature
Cedar Rapids: 73°F (22.8°C)
Sioux City: 86.5°F (30.3°C)

Average yearly rainfall
Cedar Rapids: 33.7 inches (85.6 cm)
Sioux City: 26 inches (66 cm)

Average yearly snowfall
Cedar Rapids: 30.2 inches (76.7 cm)
Sioux City: 31 inches (79 cm)

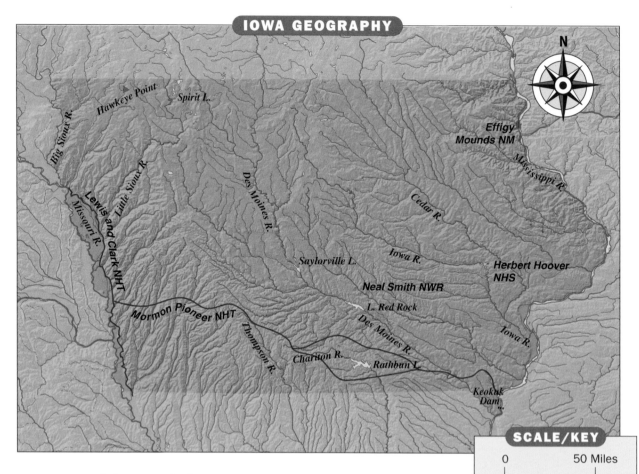

SCALE/KEY

0	50 Miles
0	50 Kilometers

NM	National Monument
NWR	National Wildlife Refuge
NHS	National Historic Site
NHT	National Historic Trail
▲	Highest Point
	Mountains

a quarter of the state's drainage. Besides rivers, Iowa offers some 90,000 acres (36,423 hectares) of lakes.

Plants and Animals

Although it has been thinly populated, Iowa has known centuries of human occupation. As a result, the seas of tall prairie grasses that once covered more than 30,000,000 acres (12,140,000 ha) of the land now only cover about 30,000 acres (12,140 ha). Ancient hardwood forests of elm, oak, hickory, maple, and walnut have been cut down over two hundred years of settlement and, more recently, by clear-cutting, the wholesale harvesting of trees. The more than 2,000,000 acres (809,400 ha) of wetlands that existed in the early eighteenth century now cover only about 35,000 acres (14,165 ha). Conservation efforts are now under way to restore the original tall grasses in certain areas; in a separate effort, the wetlands are slated for restoration.

Vast herds of buffalo once swarmed across Iowa's prairies, which provided unlimited hunting grounds for such large predators as cougars. Although most of these large animals have been wiped out, conservation efforts have increased the state's population of white-tailed deer to numbers greater than before European settlement. Conservation programs also have reintroduced such native animals as wild turkeys, river otters, and peregrine falcons. Cottontail rabbits, coyotes, foxes, and opossums are common across much of Iowa; jackrabbits live mainly on the open plains of the northwest.

Many of Iowa's native birds, including brightly colored blue jays, cardinals, and goldfinches, reside in the state year-round, thanks to the inviting habitat of Iowa's farmlands. Bluebirds, indigo buntings, orioles, and scarlet tanagers are among Iowa's seasonal songbirds. Game birds such as partridges, quail, and ring-necked pheasants are plentiful as well, partly due to the efforts of a state game-bird hatchery in Boone County. Bald eagles, once endangered by the pesticide DDT, now thrive up and down the length of the Mississippi, and ducks and geese are plentiful. Northeastern Iowa's fast-moving streams teem with smallmouth bass and hatchery trout. Bluegill, catfish, crappies, largemouth bass, northern pike, and walleye can be found in many of the state's lakes and slower streams.

Major Rivers

Mississippi River
2,340 miles
 (3,765 km) long

Missouri River
2,315 miles
 (3,725 km) long

Des Moines River
535 miles (861 km) long

Largest Lakes

Lake Red Rock
19,000 acres (7,689 ha)

Rathbun Lake
11,000 acres (4,452 ha)

Saylorville Lake
5,950 acres (2,408 ha)

▼ The lights of Sioux City are reflected in the Missouri River.

Feeding the World

> Ours is a state of good people, closely tied to the rhythms of nature with a stability and resilience that was, and still is, uncommon. We must seize this day, and fashion a future string of endless success stories; of families coming back home for good-paying jobs; of communities with new leaders and new life; of a state known for steady growth.
>
> — *former Iowa governor Terry Branstad*

Thanks to its fertile lands, abundant water, and long growing season, Iowa has long been one of the nation's foremost agricultural states. Iowa grows more corn than any other state — approximately 20 percent of the national total — and is sometimes called the Corn State. It also leads the nation in hog production, raising about a quarter of the overall U.S. total. Iowa is one of the nation's leading producers of beef cattle, soybeans, and pork. About 7 percent of the nation's food supply originates on Iowa's farms. And yet, in recent decades, manufacturing and service-related industries have taken the leading role in the state's economy.

Manufacturing

In Iowa, manufacturing and farming work hand in glove, especially in the eastern cities of Davenport and Waterloo. Corn and pork processing, meatpacking operations, and farm machinery manufacturing are but a few examples of agriculture and industry working together. Corn oil, cornstarch, corn sugar, and sugar manufacturing are important in cities such as Cedar Rapids, Clinton, Keokuk, and Muscatine. Cedar Rapids and Sioux City are leading producers of breakfast cereals and popcorn. The manufacture of farming and construction machinery ranks second among Iowa's factory activities. Davenport, Des Moines, Dubuque, and Waterloo are Iowa's foremost machinery-production sites.

Top Employers (of workers age sixteen and over)	
Services	32%
Wholesale and retail trade	22%
Manufacturing	17.5%
Agriculture, forestry, and fisheries	7.8%
Finance, insurance, real estate	6.2%
Transportation, communications, and public utilities	6.2%
Construction	4.8%
Public administration	3.4%
Mining	0.1%

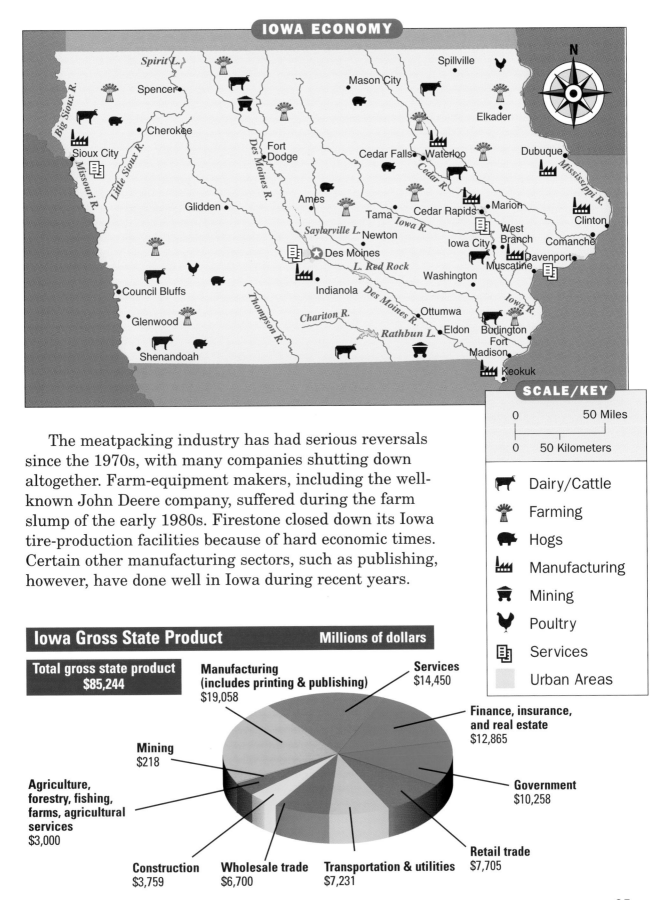

IOWA ECONOMY

The meatpacking industry has had serious reversals since the 1970s, with many companies shutting down altogether. Farm-equipment makers, including the well-known John Deere company, suffered during the farm slump of the early 1980s. Firestone closed down its Iowa tire-production facilities because of hard economic times. Certain other manufacturing sectors, such as publishing, however, have done well in Iowa during recent years.

SCALE/KEY

0 — 50 Miles

0 — 50 Kilometers

- Dairy/Cattle
- Farming
- Hogs
- Manufacturing
- Mining
- Poultry
- Services
- Urban Areas

Iowa Gross State Product — Millions of dollars

Total gross state product $85,244

- Manufacturing (includes printing & publishing) $19,058
- Services $14,450
- Finance, insurance, and real estate $12,865
- Government $10,258
- Retail trade $7,705
- Transportation & utilities $7,231
- Wholesale trade $6,700
- Construction $3,759
- Agriculture, forestry, fishing, farms, agricultural services $3,000
- Mining $218

Service, Finance, and Insurance Industries

Since World War II, Iowa's economic leaders have made a concerted effort to maintain a balance between agriculture and industry. So began Iowa's long transition from a complete reliance on farming to a more diversified economy. As automation became commonplace on Iowa's farms, urban manufacturing and service jobs drew increasing numbers of people away from agriculture. Today, services comprise the second-largest segment of Iowa's gross state product — the total annual value of a state's goods and services.

Finance and insurance, Iowa's third-most significant business sector, grew rapidly during the 1980s. A number of insurance companies, including State Farm Insurance Company and Principal Financial Group, are now located in Des Moines, making that city one of the major insurance industry centers in the United States.

Transportation

When settlers first arrived in the Iowa region, buffalo trails and hunting paths made up the only overland travel network. Iowa's first railroad began operating in 1855, and the first line to cross the entire state appeared in 1867. Today, Iowa's transportation industry is mostly dedicated to the shipping needs of farmers and factories. Crops and meat make their way to food processors via train, truck, or barge.

Starting in the 1830s, steamboat transportation on the Mississippi River also grew into a huge industry, driven by Wisconsin and Minnesota lumber companies that sold their logs to states along the river, including Iowa. This allowed Iowa's settlers to trade their sod homes for wooden frame houses. During the early years of the twentieth century, railroads and riverboats stepped up the pace, finding new markets for the state's farm products. Iowa's busiest ports are all still found on the Mississippi River.

Made in Iowa

Leading farm products and crops
Corn
Hogs
Cattle
Eggs
Milk
Soybeans

Other products
Chemicals
Electronics
Farm machinery
Processed foods

Major Airports

Airport	Location	Passengers per year (2000)
Des Moines International	Des Moines	1,749,559
Eastern Iowa	Cedar Rapids	999,951
Sioux Gateway	Sioux City	169,927

Energy and Utilities

Iowa currently derives its electrical power from several sources. About 85 percent comes from coal-burning plants, while 10 percent is generated by nuclear facilities. During recent years, Iowa has tried to produce ethanol from corn for use as a gasoline additive to decrease reliance on oil.

Modern Agriculture

Iowa still has over 90,000 farms according to a 1997 tally, which works out to about one farm for every thirty-three of the state's residents. Many smaller farms have been sold to massive agribusiness operations over the past decade, but there are still about 80,000 family farms remaining. The proportion of Iowa's lands dedicated to agriculture remains constant, at around 90 percent.

Beginning in the 1930s, Iowa's farmers became aware that over time farming damages the land. To repair the damage and to prevent future harm, Iowans began to practice such conservation techniques as terracing and contour plowing in an effort to preserve precious topsoil. Many modern Iowa farmers are turning to organic farming methods and sustainable agriculture techniques. As the twenty-first century unfolds, Iowa's future remains, as ever, tied to the earth.

Going Organic

Iowans have always been on the cutting edge of agricultural innovation. Many Iowa farmers are growing crops organically, without the help of pesticides and chemical fertilizers. Today, Iowa is the nation's top producer of organic soybeans. To guide farmers and to protect consumers, the Iowa state legislature has set up guidelines for organic farmers to follow so that the label "organic" on Iowa produce means just that.

▼ Barges pass Iowa farmland as they carry goods on the Mississippi River to and from industrial cities, such as Davenport and Dubuque.

Defending the Highest Good

> The belief that we are defending the highest good of the mothers of our race and the ultimate welfare of society makes every sacrifice seem trivial, every duty a pleasure.
>
> — *Carrie Lane Chapman Catt, 1911, social reformer and winner of the 1992 Iowa Award*

Iowa's Territorial Governor Robert Lucas tried to get Iowa admitted to the Union in 1839, but his efforts were squashed by Iowa's voters, who were unwilling to pay the salaries of state and local officials. Finally, in 1844, Iowa's voters approved a state constitution as a prelude to statehood. The U.S. Congress, however, wanted a much smaller Iowa than the voters had in mind. This dispute killed Iowa's first official attempt at statehood. Two years later, a constitutional convention in Iowa City drafted a new constitution that satisfied both Congress and Iowans — and that set the proposed state's boundaries in their present places.

Other forces thwarted Iowa's early attempts to achieve statehood. In the years leading up to the Civil War, the U.S. government tried to appease states on both sides of the slavery question by allowing slavery in some states and not in others. Congress wished to keep the number of free states and slave states in balance. This meant some states had to wait for admission until they could enter the Union in a way that kept the scales even between slave and free states. When Florida came into the Union as a slave state in 1845, Congress was able to pass a bill bringing Iowa in as a free state the following year. On December 28, 1846, President James K. Polk signed this bill into law, making Iowa the twenty-ninth state. Democrat Ansel Briggs became the new state's first governor. In 1857, Iowa moved its capital from Iowa City to the more centrally located Des Moines, where it has remained ever since.

Iowa Caucuses

The Iowa Caucuses have their roots in 1846, the year the Hawkeye State achieved statehood. During January of each presidential election year, candidates from both major parties speak at gatherings across the state such as political rallies and Rotary Club meetings. Then, on a Tuesday in February, Iowans gather in small groups, called caucuses, across 2,500 electoral precincts to decide whom they will support. Candidates who succeed in Iowa (such as Jimmy Carter in 1976) attract media attention and campaign dollars. A bad performance, however, can devastate a candidate's chances of becoming president (as occurred with Steve Forbes in 1996).

Elected Posts in the Executive Branch		
Office	Length of Term	Term Limits
Governor	4 years	none
Lieutenant Governor	4 years	none
Secretary of State	4 years	none
Treasurer	4 years	none
Attorney General	4 years	none
Auditor	4 years	none
Secretary of Agriculture	4 years	none

Iowa's Constitution

Iowa adopted its current constitution in 1857, which, among other things, finally allowed Iowans to build their own banking system. Constitutional amendments may be brought forward from either of the state legislature's two houses and must receive majority votes in both houses in two consecutive legislative sessions. Citizens also may call for a constitutional convention to propose amendments. Voters are asked once each decade whether they wish to call such a convention. A majority of the voting electorate is required both to hold a constitutional convention and then to amend the state constitution by means of a convention.

Executive Branch

Iowa's chief executive officer, the governor, is elected to a four-year term, along with a lieutenant governor. The office has no term limit. Iowa grants its governor the power to veto, or strike down, laws passed by the legislature. Iowa's lawmakers, however, are empowered to override a veto with a two-thirds majority vote in each legislative house. The leaders of about twenty state agencies are appointed by the governor. Other elected executive-branch officials include the attorney general, auditor, secretary of agriculture, secretary of state, and treasurer, all of whom serve four-year terms.

▼ The state capitol in Des Moines is topped with a dome that reaches 275 feet (84 m) and is covered in 23-karat gold leaf.

Legislative Branch

Iowa's lawmaking body, known as the General Assembly, is composed of two legislative houses: a senate with fifty members (one per senatorial district) and a house of representatives with one hundred members (one per representative district). Voters elect their state senators and representatives to four-year and two-year terms respectively. Sessions of the General Assembly begin every year on the second Monday in January and can last for up to 110 days.

Judicial Branch

The governor appoints Iowa's judges, who later must receive voter approval in order to keep their posts. Iowa's highest court is known as the supreme court. Seven justices sit on this court, where they serve eight-year terms. Other state courts are the courts of appeals and district courts. The terms of all judges on these courts are six years. Each district court has anywhere from seven to twenty-eight judges. Associate judges, who serve four-year terms, handle less-urgent cases.

Local Government

Boards of supervisors run each of Iowa's ninety-nine counties. These boards usually consist of three elected members each serving four-year terms. The majority of Iowa's cities are governed by a mayor and city council. Others employ a city council and city manager instead. Iowa's constitution was amended in 1968 to permit the state's cities to practice home rule, the authority to adopt their own governmental charters.

Revenue

Approximately 55 percent of Iowa's income, or general revenue, comes from taxes paid by individuals and corporations, as well as from a state sales tax and certain fees charged for government services. Other revenues come from taxes on motor-vehicle licenses, motor fuels, insurance, and inheritances.

A Heartbeat Away

Henry Agard Wallace (1888-1965) was an Iowa native raised on an Adair County farm. Wallace studied under George Washington Carver at Iowa State University, where he became an expert in plant genetics, and subsequently introduced high-yield varieties of hybrid corn to Iowa's farmers. President Franklin D. Roosevelt appointed him secretary of agriculture in 1933. In this post, Wallace helped develop programs to bring electricity and economic relief to Depression-devastated rural Iowans. He also introduced soil conservation programs and farm price supports to aid downtrodden farmers. In 1940, Wallace became Roosevelt's running mate and, in 1941, became vice president. He served a single term as vice president, then lost a bid for the presidency on the Progressive party ticket in 1948.

General Assembly			
House	Number of Members	Length of Term	Term Limits
Senate	50 senators	4 years	none
House of Representatives	100 representatives	2 years	none

HERBERT HOOVER (1929–1933)
Born August 10, 1874, in West Branch, Iowa, Herbert Clark Hoover was a blacksmith's son. He was orphaned at the age of nine and was subsequently raised by an uncle in Oregon. Hoover graduated with a degree in mine engineering, then worked as a mine laborer in California before being hired to run a new gold-mining operation in Australia. Over the next twenty years, he grew wealthy from mining ventures he began in Africa, Asia, and Europe. The horrendous violence of World War I (1914–1918) was an affront to Hoover's peace-loving Quaker beliefs and motivated him to devote his life to public service. Hoover headed relief organizations that distributed food in Europe.

Hoover became the U.S. food administrator under President Woodrow Wilson during World War I and was also director of the London-based American Relief Administration, an agency that helped Europeans caught in the war's crossfire. From 1921 to 1928, Hoover served as secretary of commerce under Presidents Warren G. Harding and Calvin Coolidge. In 1928, he was elected the nation's thirty-first president, the first U.S. president born west of the Mississippi River. After the stock market crash of 1929 rocked the United States, Hoover and his Republican free-market policies were blamed for the subsequent Great Depression. Hoover remained a critic of his successor, Franklin D. Roosevelt, and Roosevelt's economic policies. Hoover died in New York City on October 20, 1964.

Party Politics

Iowa's earliest settlers tended to back the Democratic party. Iowa achieved statehood in 1846, and, by the mid-1850s, many of the state's Democrats had become disenchanted with their party's failure to oppose the practice of slavery. These Democrats helped create Iowa's Republican party. Republicans gained command of state politics in 1858 with the election of Governor Ralph P. Lowe. For the next one hundred years, most of Iowa's governors were Republicans.

The state's legislative districts were redrawn in the mid-1960s. As a result, representation of urban areas increased, which had the effect of placing more Democrats in the state legislature. Beginning in 1970, Iowa has redrawn its legislative districts every ten years, with each federal census, to ensure fair representation. Modern-day Iowa is effectively a two-party state in which a variety of viewpoints can be heard.

Just Passing Through

Richard M. Nixon, the nation's thirty-seventh president, was stationed in Iowa during World War II at the Naval Reserve Aviation Base in Ottumwa. Ronald Reagan, the fortieth U.S. president, worked as a sportscaster for two Des Moines radio stations, WHO and WOC, from 1933 until 1937.

Songs of the Prairie

> Go read the story of thy past,
> Iowa, O! Iowa
> What glorious deeds, what fame thou hast!
> Iowa, O! Iowa
>
> — *"The Song of Iowa," lyrics by S. H. M. Byers,*
> *sung to "Der Tannenbaum"*

A s the 1957 hit musical *The Music Man* by Mason City's Meredith Willson demonstrates, Iowans love a good tune. Not surprisingly, the Hawkeye State has spawned its fair share of world-class musicians in a wide variety of styles. Swing-era bandleader Glenn Miller (1904–1944) was a native of Clarinda, and jazz legend Bix Beiderbecke (1903–1931) hailed from Davenport. Early rock-and-roll stars Phil and Don Everly, better known as the Everly Brothers, began making live radio performances with their parents in the 1950s at Shenandoah's station KMA. Avoca-born actor-singer Richard Beymer (1938–) portrayed Tony in the 1961 movie version of Leonard Bernstein's and Stephen Sondheim's musical *West Side Story*.

Iowa also has a long-standing association with classical music. Romantic-era composer Antonín Dvořák (1841–1904) was born in Bohemia (now part of the Czech Republic), but Iowa had a tremendous impact on one of his most famous works. Dvořák spent the summer of 1893 in the small Iowa town of Spillville, enjoying its Bohemian community. During his stay, Dvořák revised his Ninth Symphony in E Minor, op. 95, which was subtitled *From the New World*. This classic work is most often referred to simply as the *New World* symphony. Today, symphony orchestras in several of Iowa's largest cities keep Iowa's classical music tradition alive. The Hawkeye State is home to eighteen music and dance associations, sixty-five theater groups, and eighty arts agencies.

▲ Iowan Glenn Miller was one of the best-known and best-loved bandleaders of the 1930s and 1940s.

Painting, Sculpture, and the Graphic Arts

The painter most closely identified with Iowa is Grant Wood (1892–1942). Wood applied classic, realistic techniques to themes that evoked the rural Iowa experience. He premiered his most recognized work, *American Gothic*, in 1930 at the Art Institute of Chicago. The farmhouse he used as a model still stands in the rural town of Eldon. In 1932, Wood founded an art colony at Stone City. Iowa sculptor Nellie Verne Walker (1874–1973) of Red Oak built a long and distinguished career creating giant works of art out of stone. Among Iowa's best-known recent and contemporary artists are Dennis Ashbaugh, Paula Elliott, Thomas Gormally, Dennis Kardon, and Kim Uchiyama.

Literature

The University of Iowa, in Iowa City, is home to the most famous workshop for writers in the nation and possibly the world. The Program in Creative Writing, known as the Iowa Writers' Workshop, opened in 1936 and has grown steadily in prestige since then. Published writers teach at and visit the university to read their own works and to offer criticism and advice to graduate student writers. The program is dedicated to the development of creative writing, both fiction and poetry, and has graduated many of the best-known authors in the country. Faculty and visiting writers have included such outstanding U.S. writers as Frank Conroy, Robert Penn Warren, John Irving, and Kurt Vonnegut.

Novelist, short-story writer, and essayist Hamlin Garland (1860–1940) became one of Iowa's first successful fiction writers. In short-story collections such as *Main-Travelled Roads* (1891) and novels such as *Rose of Dutcher's Coolly* (1895), he presented a realistic view of life in rural America. Ruth Suckow (1892–1960) worked in a similar storytelling vein. Her novels included *Country People* (1924) and *The Folks* (1934). Colfax native James Norman Hall (1887–1951) authored the well-known seagoing tale *Mutiny on the Bounty* (1932),

The Day the Music Died

Among the most influential figures in the early history of rock-and-roll music were Buddy Holly, Ritchie Valens, and J. P. Richardson, who was better known as the "Big Bopper." During the cold winter of 1959, these three rock legends were touring and performing across the Midwest. On the morning of February 3, following a performance at the Surf Ballroom in Clear Lake, a small plane carrying the three rockers took off from Mason City, bound for the next show on their tour. Tragically, the hazardous weather conditions caused the plane to crash just outside Clear Lake, and everyone on board was killed.

▶ The Cedar Rapids Museum of Art houses the world's biggest collection of the works of Iowan Grant Wood.

of which three films have been made. Ladora-born Mildred Wirt Benson (1905–2002) was one of the first of many authors who wrote novels in the Nancy Drew mystery series. She authored more than 130 books during her long career. Davenport-born playwright and novelist Susan Glaspell (1882–1948) won the Pulitzer Prize for drama in 1931 for her play *Alison's House* (1930).

Outdoor Iowa

Iowa is dotted with more than eighty state parks where residents and visitors can enjoy the state's great natural beauty. Many of the parks are located on historic sites, providing both relaxation and education. One such site, Preparation Canyon in western Iowa, is on the site of what was once a village founded by a group of Mormons in the 1850s. The park includes 344 acres (139 ha) for hikers and picnickers.

Maquoketa Caves in the eastern part of the state are full of natural beauty and historic interest. Archaeologists have discovered material evidence, such as arrow points, suggesting that the caves have been popular for many centuries. The largest of the caves is the 1,100-square

DID YOU KNOW?

The United States Postal Service chose *Young Corn* (1931), an image created by Iowa painter Grant Wood, to adorn the 1996 postage stamp commemorating the 150th anniversary of the Hawkeye State's entry into the Union.

▼ Sports enthusiasts make the most of Iowa's winters. The Winter Games of the University of Okoboji (which does not really exist) offer many activities, including broomball (similar to ice hockey) and dogsled racing.

foot (102-sq m) Dancehall Cave, which has walkways and electric lighting. Other caves are of all shapes and sizes, and while visitors can stroll into some, they must crawl into others. Among the many interesting limestone formations in the area of the caves is a natural bridge that stands about 50 feet (15 m) high and spans a creek.

In northeastern Iowa, Effigy Mounds National Monument is a park that includes the remains of one of Iowa's earliest civilizations. The spectacular 2,526-acre (1,022-ha) park includes 195 mounds, 31 of which are in the shapes of animals, such as lizards, birds, and bears.

Sports

Many Iowans are avid fans of the University of Iowa's football team, the Hawkeyes. The team is part of the Big Ten Conference and, in recent years, has had a number of its quarterbacks named all-Big Ten athletes. Over the many years that the Hawkeyes have been playing football, they also have had many all-American players. In 1935, Iowan Jay Berwanger, who played for the University of Chicago in Illinois, became the first person to win a Heisman Trophy.

Baseball also has been important to Iowans as far back as the Civil War, when the workers in coal-mining towns organized themselves into amateur teams. Baseball history was made in Des Moines in 1930 when the Des Moines Demons beat the Wichita Aviators in the world's first night baseball game under permanent lights. Today, baseball enthusiasts can visit the Dyersville baseball diamond used in the 1989 film *Field of Dreams*.

Basketball fans in the state can choose from many teams in the National College Athletic Association. Iowa State University, the University of Iowa, and the University of Northern Iowa all have both men's and women's teams. In Des Moines, fans can attend games of the Dragons, who are part of the International Basketball Association.

The track competition at Drake University in Des Moines draws thousands of enthusiastic fans every year. One of the

▼ Iowa Hawkeyes guard Luke Recker (*right*) looks to pass the basketball around Indiana University center Jeff Newton. Recker's field goal at the buzzer was the game-winning shot over Indiana in the semifinals of the 2002 Big Ten Conference Men's Basketball Tournament.

most famous names in track and field, Bruce Jenner, attended Graceland College in Lamoni. Jenner entered Graceland as a football, basketball, and track star, but an injury soon turned him to the decathlon. In 1976, he won the Olympic decathlon in Montreal. Jenner's picture then appeared on the Wheaties cereal box, making his face familiar to breakfasters all over the United States.

Iowa's flat terrain makes bicycle racing a popular pursuit; every spring and summer dozens of bike racers test their skill and stamina in towns across the state. The RAGBRAI, the *Des Moines Register*'s Annual Great Bicycle Ride Across Iowa, lasts seven days and draws participants from all over the world. The Tour de Poweshiek (of Poweshiek County) and Burlington's Criterium are among Iowa's other high-profile bike races. Skiers and snowboarders enjoy the heart-stopping thrills offered by the steep slopes of Iowa's "Little Switzerland" area in the northeast.

Museums

Iowa has many museums. The world's largest collection of Grant Wood paintings can be found in the Cedar Rapids Museum of Art. Cherokee is home to the Sanford Museum and Planetarium, which features archaeological, astronomical, and geological exhibits. In Davenport, the Putnam Museum of History and Natural Science concentrates on local and regional history. The Des Moines Art Center displays American and European paintings and sculptures, and the State Historical Museum in the same city highlights Iowa history. The Science Center of Iowa, also in Des Moines, focuses on developments

▲ Iowans enjoy cross-country skiing (*above*) in winter and baseball (*inset*) all summer long. The baseball field pictured here was used in the movie *Field of Dreams,* which celebrated one Iowan's love of the game.

in science and technology, while Waterloo's Grout Museum of History and Science concentrates on Native American culture and pioneer life. Not to be forgotten, the town of West Branch in Cedar County is home to the Herbert Hoover National Historic Site, which includes the presidential library and museum.

The Iowa Award

Iowa honors its distinguished citizens with the Iowa Award. The Iowa Centennial Memorial Foundation established the award, the Hawkeye State's highest citizen honor, in 1948. It is bestowed on Iowans who have made outstanding achievements in their fields and is given out approximately every five years. President Herbert Hoover received the first Iowa Award in 1951. Other recipients include feminist reformer Carrie Lane Chapman Catt, former U.S. vice president Henry A. Wallace, agricultural scientist Norman E. Borlaug, pollster George Gallup, physicist James A. Van Allen, and composer Meredith Willson. As a state that has always championed education and individual freedoms, it is not surprising that Iowa has made so many proud cultural contributions, both to the nation and the world.

▼ At the Family Museum of Arts and Science in Bettendorf, visitors can touch a tornado, make music, and explore the workings of the human heart.

Iowa Individuals

Much of the Iowa farm lore concerns the coming of company. When the rooster crows in the doorway, or the cat licks his fur, company is on the way.

— Iowa: A Guide to the Hawkeye State, *1938*

Following are only a few of the thousands of people who were born, died, or spent much of their lives in Iowa and made extraordinary contributions to the state and the nation.

BLACK HAWK
NATIVE AMERICAN CHIEF
BORN: *1767, near present-day Rock Island, IL*
DIED: *October 1838, near the Des Moines River*

Born Ma-ka-tai-me-she-kia-kiak (Black Sparrow Hawk), Black Hawk became a warrior at the age of fifteen when he helped his Sauk people fight the Osage. An independent, strong-willed man, Black Hawk rejected both the settlers' alcohol and Christianity. In 1795, Black Hawk signed the Treaty of Greenville, which offered the Sauk people U.S. protection. After an 1804 skirmish with the Sauk, the U.S. government used alcohol to induce a few Sauk leaders to sign a peace agreement that ceded Sauk land in Illinois, Wisconsin, and Missouri in exchange for a tiny amount of cash. Black Hawk and other Sauk chiefs challenged the treaty without

success. Black Hawk's people sided with the British during the War of 1812. In 1828, the federal government forced the Sauk into Iowa. In 1832, Black Hawk tried to reclaim his people's lands, which resulted in bloody clashes with the U.S. Army and Black Hawk's capture. After the fighting, known as the Black Hawk War, Black Hawk became a celebrity. Black Hawk died in his Iowa lodge, a few months after his final public appearance.

AMELIA JENKS BLOOMER
SOCIAL REFORMER
BORN: *May 27, 1818, Homer, NY*
DIED: *December 30, 1894, Council Bluffs*

In 1849, Amelia Jenks Bloomer became the founder and editor of *The Lily,* perhaps the first U.S. magazine published for, and produced by, women. The magazine dealt with temperance, or avoiding alcohol; women's suffrage and equal rights; and issues of morality. The magazine ceased publication when Bloomer moved to Council Bluffs in 1855. There, she became president of the Iowa Woman Suffrage Association. One of the pioneering feminists of her day, Bloomer also influenced women's fashion in the latter half of the nineteenth century by adopting a short-skirt-and-baggy-pants outfit, introduced by Elizabeth Smith Miller. Bloomer wore this garment during her public appearances campaigning for temperance and women's suffrage. It came to be called the "bloomer" and eventually became a symbol of feminism.

"BUFFALO BILL" CODY
FRONTIERSMAN
BORN: *February 26, 1846, LeClaire*
DIED: *January 10, 1917, Denver, CO*

The man who would become a Wild West legend, William Frederick Cody, was born in Iowa and lived there until he moved to Kansas with his family in the 1850s. As a young man, Cody carried messages for the Pony Express, served in the Union Army in the Civil War, and supplied buffalo meat to Kansas Pacific Railroad workers in 1867 and 1868. During this period, Cody became known as "Buffalo Bill." He took part in several skirmishes against Native Americans while serving as the Fifth U.S. Cavalry's chief scout. In 1869, Cody's life became the subject of a dime novel, and he became famous as a result. Cody appeared for more than a decade in touring stage melodramas, and, in 1883, he developed a Wild West show, thrilling U.S. and European audiences with re-creations of roundups, stagecoach robberies, and battles against Native Americans. Cody's show made stars of such Wild West gunslingers as Annie Oakley and Buck Taylor. Cody retired in 1913.

CARRIE LANE CHAPMAN CATT
REFORMER
BORN: *January 9, 1859, Ripon, WI*
DIED: *March 9, 1947, New Rochelle, NY*

Carrie Lane moved to Iowa when she was seven. She worked her way through Iowa State College (now Iowa State University). Following graduation, she worked at a variety of jobs, including teacher, school superintendent, and reporter. She joined the Iowa Woman Suffrage Association in 1887 and was soon working at the national level for the suffrage cause. Carrie Lane Chapman Catt's extraordinary ability to organize people made her one of the first feminists to take decisive political action on behalf of women's rights. After her first term as president of the National American Woman Suffrage Association (NAWSA) ended in 1904, she went on to become president of the International Woman Suffrage Alliance before becoming president of the NAWSA once again. As president, Catt played a major role in the passage of the Nineteenth Amendment to the U.S. Constitution. Passed in 1920, the amendment gave women the right to vote. That same year, Catt established the League of

Women Voters. Five years later, she founded the Committee on the Cause and Cure of War. She continued to work tirelessly for peace for the remainder of her life.

HAMLIN GARLAND
WRITER

BORN: *September 14, 1860, West Salem, WI*
DIED: *March 4, 1940, Hollywood, CA*

Hannibal Hamlin Garland grew up on farms in Wisconsin and Iowa and later became one of the most influential writers of the American realist style. Garland was perhaps the first successful author associated with the Hawkeye State. Garland's best-known works include the 1891 short-story collection *Main-Travelled Roads* and its 1910 sequel, *Other Main-Travelled Roads,* a compilation of stories from two earlier collections. He also is regarded as a master of the novel, winning fame for *Rose of Dutcher's Coolly* (1895), a harsh depiction of life in the rural Midwest. He was particularly sensitive to the oppression endured by Iowa's women. Garland wrote two autobiographical novels, *A Son of the Middle Border* (1917) and *A Daughter of the Middle Border* (1921), for which he won the 1922 Pulitzer Prize for biography. Garland has been called "the first actual farmer in American fiction."

GRANT WOOD
PAINTER

BORN: *February 13, 1892, Anamosa*
DIED: *February 12, 1942, Iowa City*

American regionalist painter Grant Wood earned wide acclaim during the 1930s for his beautiful portraits of life and nature in rural America. While visiting Europe during the late 1920s, Wood was inspired by the works of the van Eyck brothers and other Flemish masters. Wood adapted this style to the depiction of the themes of the American Midwest. Wood's best-known paintings include *American Gothic* (1930) and *Daughters of Revolution* (1932). For *American Gothic,* which depicts a dour-faced, pitchfork-toting farmer standing beside his daughter, Wood used a pair of live models: his own sister, Nan, and Dr. B. H. McKeeby, a Cedar Rapids dentist. Like other American regionalist painters, such as John Steuart Curry and Thomas Hart Benton, Wood spurned modernism in favor of more classical, representational styles.

MEREDITH WILLSON
COMPOSER

BORN: *May 18, 1902, Mason City*
DIED: *June 15, 1984, Santa Monica, CA*

Best known as the composer and lyricist of the 1957 smash Broadway musical *The Music Man,* which is set in a small town in Iowa, Willson began his musical career playing the flute in John Philip Sousa's famous band from 1921 to 1923. Willson later played with the New York

Philharmonic Orchestra. During the early 1930s, he served as a musical director at NBC in San Francisco and concert director for KFRC radio. Later that decade, Willson relocated to Hollywood, where he directed the music for many NBC radio shows and composed musical scores for films. During the 1940s, he was twice nominated for an Academy Award. During World War II, Willson joined the army and helped operate the Armed Forces Radio Service. Many of Willson's songs have become standards, including "It's Beginning to Look a Lot Like Christmas," "May the Good Lord Bless and Keep You," "Seventy-six Trombones," "You and I," and "Till There Was You," which became a major hit for the Beatles in 1963. Willson also wrote the music and lyrics for the 1960 musical *The Unsinkable Molly Brown*.

BIX BEIDERBECKE
JAZZ MUSICIAN
BORN: *March 10, 1903, Davenport*
DIED: *August 7, 1931, New York, NY*

Leon Bismarck "Bix" Beiderbecke is widely regarded as the greatest white jazz musician of the 1920s. Beiderbecke played both the cornet and piano and also wrote music. He exerted a tremendous influence on later generations of jazz players. A self-taught cornetist, Beiderbecke played to wide acclaim in Chicago's jazz clubs while still a teenager. In 1923, he joined a jazz combo called the Wolverines, where he met Jimmy McPartland, one of his most famous musical protegés. Beiderbecke's style was characterized by his laid-back, warm tone, which contrasted with the more dramatic style of Louis Armstrong, his musical mentor. Among Beiderbecke's most highly regarded compositions are "In a Mist," "Candlelights," and "In the Dark." Each July, Beiderbecke's legacy is remembered at Davenport's Bix Beiderbecke Memorial Jazz Festival. Beiderbecke died at the young age of twenty-eight of alcoholism and pneumonia.

JOHN WAYNE
ACTOR
BORN: *May 26, 1907, Winterset*
DIED: *June 11, 1979, Los Angeles, CA*

Born Marion Michael Morrison, actor John Wayne (*left*) came to represent the epitome of the tough, self-reliant hero of the nineteenth-century American frontier through the roles he played in twentieth-century movies. Wayne appeared in more than 150 films, many of which were directed by the famous director John Ford. Ford's 1939 Western *Stagecoach* catapulted Wayne to international stardom. Wayne also gave memorable performances in *She Wore a Yellow Ribbon* (1949), *Red River* (1948), *The Searchers* (1956), and *Rio Bravo* (1959). John Wayne received an Academy Award for *True Grit* (1969), in which he portrayed a crusty, aging Western gunfighter. Wayne starred in a number of films in other genres as well, including John Ford's *The Long Voyage Home* (1940), *They Were Expendable* (1945), and *The Quiet Man* (1952). Wayne both starred in and directed *The Alamo* (1960) and *The Green Berets* (1968).

Iowa

History At-A-Glance

1673
French explorer Louis Jolliet and missionary Jacques Marquette become the first Europeans to see the Iowa region.

1682
The Mississippi River Valley is claimed for France by René-Robert Cavelier, Sieur de La Salle; La Salle names it Louisiana.

1788
French-Canadian Julien Dubuque, Iowa's first non-Native settler, starts mining lead on land located near the modern-day city of Dubuque.

1808
The U.S. Army establishes its first military outpost in Iowa, Fort Madison.

1832
U.S. troops defeat the Sauk and Mesquakie in the Black Hawk War; the tribes are then forced from their eastern Iowa lands.

1846
Iowa approves a constitution and enters the Union as the 29th state.

1857
The Iowa legislature adopts the state's present-day constitution; Des Moines becomes the state's capital.

1867
The first trans-Iowa railroad is completed, running from the Mississippi River to Council Bluffs.

1868
Iowa amends its constitution to give African-American men the right to vote.

1873
Iowa farmers oppose excessive freight charges by railroads; freight reforms come the following year.

1884
Construction is completed on the state capitol in Des Moines.

1913
Construction of the Keokuk Dam is complete.

1600   **1700**   **1800**

1492
Christopher Columbus comes to New World.

1607
Capt. John Smith and three ships land on Virginia coast and start first English settlement in New World — Jamestown.

1754–63
French and Indian War.

1773
Boston Tea Party.

1776
Declaration of Independence adopted July 4.

1777
Articles of Confederation adopted by Continental Congress.

1787
U.S. Constitution written.

1812–14
War of 1812.

United States
History At-A-Glance

1917
Iowa initiates a large-scale road-building program.

1920s
Low prices for agricultural products cause many Iowa farmers to default on their mortgages and lose their land; high-yield corn introduced in Iowa.

1928
Herbert Hoover, an Iowa native, wins the presidency of the United States.

1936
The Iowa Writers' Workshop is established at the University of Iowa.

1940
Iowan Henry Wallace is elected vice president of the United States under President Franklin D. Roosevelt.

1960
The number of city-dwelling Iowans exceeds the state's rural population for the first time.

1965
The death penalty is prohibited in Iowa.

1970
Iowa begins reapportioning its legislative districts based on the U.S. Census.

1970s
Agriculture is surpassed by manufacturing in economic importance for the first time in Iowa.

1985
Iowa establishes a state lottery to increase revenues; an executive order halts farm foreclosures for a one-year period.

1989
Iowa legalizes riverboat gambling.

1993
Heavy rains cause the worst floods in Iowa's history; crop and property damage total more than $2 billion.

1800   **1900**   **2000**

1848
Gold discovered in California draws eighty thousand prospectors in the 1849 Gold Rush.

1861–65
Civil War.

1869
Transcontinental railroad completed.

1917–18
U.S. involvement in World War I.

1929
Stock market crash ushers in Great Depression.

1941–45
U.S. involvement in World War II.

1950–53
U.S. fights in the Korean War.

1964–73
U.S. involvement in Vietnam War.

2000
George W. Bush wins the closest presidential election in history.

2001
A terrorist attack in which four hijacked airliners crash into New York City's World Trade Center, the Pentagon, and farmland in western Pennsylvania leaves thousands dead or injured.

▼ A gravel train transports gravel for local roads in Manchester, Iowa, in 1913.

Photo by:—

Festivals and Fun for All

Check web site for exact date and directions.

▲ Iowans enjoy the annual state fair.

Bix Beiderbecke Memorial Jazz Festival, Davenport

As July draws to a close, thousands of jazz enthusiasts and many performing bands gather to celebrate the life and musical legacy of the famed cornetist and composer Bix Beiderbecke in his birthplace. www.bixsociety.org

Covered Bridge Festival, Madison County

Held during the second full weekend in October, the Covered Bridge Festival brings local residents and visitors together under the burnished fall colors to celebrate the county's historic covered bridges. The event features music, demonstrations of old-time crafts, a wide array of food vendors, an antique vehicle parade, a spelling bee, and more. www.madisoncounty.com/bridge_fest.html

Fort Atkinson Rendezvous, Fort Atkinson

During the final weekend of each September, Fort Atkinson's expert staff re-creates a "frontier rendezvous," setting up about 140 tepees and lean-tos. Buckskin-clad docents (posing as 1840s-era fur trappers and traders) demonstrate the skills that kept Iowa's frontiersmen alive. Other attractions include food and craft vendors. www.silosandsmokestacks.org/resources/FieldTrip Guide/Winneshiek/fort_atkinson_military_post.htm

Grant Wood Art Festival, Stone City

On the second Sunday of each June, Stone City, Anamosa, and the surrounding areas live up to their reputation as "Grant Wood Country" by hosting the Grant Wood Art Festival. This event promotes art appreciation and education and honors the memory of Iowa painter Grant Wood, who was so enthralled with the natural beauty of the region that he established an art colony and school here during the 1930s. Attractions include art exhibits, live family entertainment, and displays of restored buildings from the art colony. www.grantwoodartfestival.org

Holzfest, Amana Colonies

Each August, the Amana Colonies play host to the biggest woodworking show in the Midwest. Visitors can enjoy diverse displays of wooden crafts, as well as ethnic food, dance, and music. www.jeonet.com/amanas/events/low_events.html

Iowa State Fair, Des Moines

Held each August, the Iowa State Fair is one of the Hawkeye State's signature annual events, drawing enormous crowds from all over the Midwest and beyond. Among the fair's many attractions are agricultural and industrial exhibits, as well as amusement park-style rides, carnival games, and much more. www.iowastatefair.com

National Balloon Classic, Indianola
Early August ushers in one of Iowa's highest-flying events. Among the many attractions are a 5-kilometer road race, hot-air balloon rides, displays of odd-shaped balloons, bathtub races, car and craft shows, night balloon-flying events, and a parade. Tethered balloon rides are available for those who want to stay connected to the ground.
www.national balloonclassic.com

National Hobo Convention, Britt
Early August brings a celebration of the footloose ways of the hobo. This gathering has taken place every August since 1900. Visitors to downtown Britt also can enjoy the permanent Hobo Museum, as well as such historic landmarks as the Armstrong House and the Hancock County Courthouse, both of which are listed on the National Register of Historic Places. Outdoor enthusiasts can enjoy the area's many parks and lakes.
www.iowatourism.org/cgi-bin/county.pl?4

Register's Annual Great Bicycle Ride Across Iowa (RAGBRAI)
The world's oldest touring bicycle ride, RAGBRAI brings its participants into close contact with Iowa's scenic wonders. The route varies from year to year, encouraging riders from all over the nation and more than a dozen foreign countries to keep returning to this annual celebration of Iowa's vibrant outdoor life.
www.ragbrai.org

Riverboat Days, Clinton
Iowa's largest July Fourth celebration comes each year to Clinton's Riverfront Park, along with fleets of Mississippi River boats. Among the many family events are a circus, a bike-board-and-blade stunt show, yo-yo demonstrations, a petting zoo, pony rides, puppet shows, scenic train rides, a craft show, bingo, a parabounce, a giant swing, a paintball booth, theater productions, magicians, hypnotists, and a flea market.
www.riverboatdays.org/home.htm

Tri-State Rodeo, Fort Madison
The start of September heralds one of the largest rodeo events in the state. In addition to the rodeo and roping events is the annual Miss Rodeo Iowa Pageant, which includes competitions in horsemanship.
www.fortmadison.com/rodeo/default.htm

University of Okoboji Winter Games, Okoboji
Late each January, Okoboji's State Pier and the surrounding areas host some forty assorted winter games and other activities, including a broomball tournament, go-kart rides across the winter ice, and dogsledding.
www.siouxland.net /siouxland/sports/okoboji_games.cfm

Victorian "Christmas Stroll," Albia
Each December, thousands of visitors are drawn to Albia's celebration of its nineteenth-century heritage. Featured attractions include an evening stroll past the town's ninety-two period buildings, a guided tour of historic landmarks, horse-drawn carriage rides, a Victorian fashion show, and "living Christmas cards" in which members of the community portray Santa Claus, elves, Ebenezer Scrooge, and other traditional Christmas characters in more than fifty of downtown Albia's storefront windows.
www.albia.com

Books

Clinton, Susan. *Herbert Hoover: Thirty-First President of the United States*. Chicago, IL: Children's Press, 1988. A detailed biography of the only U.S. president to hail from the Hawkeye State.

Duggleby, John. *Artist in Overalls: The Life of Grant Wood*. San Francisco, CA: Chronicle Books, 1996. An examination of the art and life of Grant Wood, one of the United States's most admired painters.

Fichter, George S. *First Steamboat Down the Mississippi*. Gretna, LA: Pelican, 1989. A chronicle of Iowa's territorial and early statehood periods.

LaDoux, Rita C. *Iowa*. Minneapolis, MN: Lerner Publications, 1992. A good general history of the Hawkeye State.

Thompson, Kathleen. *Iowa*. Milwaukee, WI: Raintree/Steck Vaughn, 1996. Another general history of Iowa and its people.

Witteman, Barbara. *Zebulon Pike: Soldier and Explorer*. Mankato, MN: Bridgestone Books, 2002. A book about the life and adventures of Zebulon Pike, who explored Iowa in 1805.

Web Sites

▶ Official state web site
www.state.ia.us

▶ The official web site of the Hawkeye State's capital city
www.ci.des-moines.ia.us

▶ Web site of the State Historical Society of Iowa
www.iowahistory.org

Note: Page numbers in *italics* refer to maps, illustrations, or photographs.